THE WONDERFUL WORLD OF WORDS

The BE Family

Dr Lubna Alsagoff
PhD (Stanford)

Marshall Cavendish
Children

The BE verbs were a very busy family of verbs.

There were eight BE verbs — Mama be along with her seven children.

2

The BE verbs were very friendly with many different words.

is happy   be   good   was   jumping

being   tired   were   carpenters

are   boys

am   walking   been   there

In sentences, we can use BE verbs with nouns.

We are sailors!

BE verbs can also be used with adjectives.

I am hungry!

We are hungry too!

3

We can also combine BE verbs with other verbs. The sailors are eating all the cookies!

The cook is chasing the sailors out of the kitchen!

Alas, all the king's cookies have been eaten!

Draw lines to show which **BE** verbs can be used with the different pronouns.

I

you

it

we

they

she

he

am

is

are

was

were

The **BE** verbs are playing hide-and-seek! Help me find them.

```
I  M  W  P  Z  B  P  B
S  G  A  E  E  J  S  E
P  H  C  I  R  G  I  E
J  D  N  Z  C  E  K  N
X  G  W  F  C  V  Q  H
W  A  S  J  W  G  E  X
E  B  S  C  M  R  F  R
I  W  S  R  A  Y  X  B
```

5

Can you please _____ quiet? We ___ trying to get some sleep!

But now we _____ all awake!

I _____ _____ quiet! As quiet as woodpeckers can _____!

Mr Woodpecker, I _____ very sleepy! Can you please peck on another tree?

One day, **being** came home from the library looking very sad.

What's wrong?

Look at what these grammar books say, Mama.

Verbs are **doing**, **saying** and **thinking** words.

Doing verb: The sloth climbs trees.

Saying verb: The angry bird shouted loudly.

Thinking verb: The king wondered where the queen was.

We don't do any of those things. So, are we verbs, Mama?

Of course, we are. But we are verbs that show how things are or how they are linked to one another.

We are needed in many sentences!

Examples of sentences with BE verbs:

I am very happy with my new shoes.

She is my teacher.

Farmer Sam and my mother are friends.

All the children were in school.

I think that BE verbs are like the = sign in math.

=

I am very happy with my new shoes.

=

She is my teacher.

=

Farmer Sam and my mother are friends.

=

All the children were in school.

9

been

Cappy **is** sleeping very soundly so don't wake her.

The soldiers **are** guarding the castle.

Farmer Sam **was** talking to Robbie the Robot.

Those letters **were** written by Maddie.

The chickens **were** sleeping in the chicken coop.

Without us, there would be many broken and bad sentences!

✗ I am very happy with my new shoes.

✗ She is my teacher.

✗ Farmer Sam and my mother are friends.

✗ All the children were in school.

✗ Cappy is sleeping very soundly so don't wake her.

✗ The soldiers are guarding the castle.

✗ Farmer Sam was taking Robbie the Robot for a drive.

✗ Those letters were written by Maddie.

✗ The chickens were sleeping in the chicken coop.

You are all quite right! Let's go and see Queen Verb. She'll know how to help us.

Queen Verb was in the grand throne room with the king.

She was so happy to see Mama **be** and her children.

Hello, Mama **be**. How are you and your children doing?

She had to find the WOW Grammar Book.

THE WOW GRAMMAR BOOK

Once she could correct the WOW Grammar Book, all the other grammar books would show that the **BE** family were also verbs.

Verbs

BE Family

is — am — are — being — be

was — were — been

The queen summoned the soldiers of WOW.

They searched the castle for the WOW Grammar Book.

They looked everywhere in WOW Castle. But the WOW Grammar Book was nowhere to be found!

The Fabulous Forest of WOW

In the Forest of WOW, the animals were enjoying meeting one another now that everyone was well.

At lunch, the princess told Donkey, Owl, Squirrel, Rabbit and Magpie how King Noun and Queen Verb helped the people of WOW.

16

A long time ago, a purple cloud appeared in WOW and made many citizens unwell.

The king and queen found a special book.

It helped the citizens of WOW get well!

Just as the Princess had finished telling her story, they heard a rustling behind the trees.

It was the king and queen of WOW!

Hello, Daughter!

The king and queen explained why they were there.

Owl, Squirrel and Rabbit told the king and queen what had happened in the forest of WOW and how they used the WOW Grammar Book to help the animals.

Owl returned the WOW Grammar Book to the king and queen.

Immediately, the queen sat down and took out her quill.

She turned to the chapter on verbs. She began to write.

Verbs

Doing verb

Thinking verb

Saying verb

Be verb

BE are a special family of verbs in English.
There are eight BE verbs:

Verb	How they are used
be	base form
been	-en form
being	-ing form
am	present tense used with the pronoun 'I'
is	singular present tense
are	plural present tense
was	singular past tense
were	plural past tense

Mama be and her children were so happy to be included as verbs in the WOW Grammar Book!

Dear Parents,

In this volume, children are introduced to BE verbs. These are probably the most common verbs, but they are not typical verbs. Most grammar books for young learners say verbs are action words. Some books may also include saying verbs or thinking verbs. BE verbs are different. They really are like the = sign in math, and are used to talk about the state of things and to link information in a sentence.

There are many things to be learnt about BE verbs. This volume provides a good start to your child's learning journey!

Page	Possible Answers

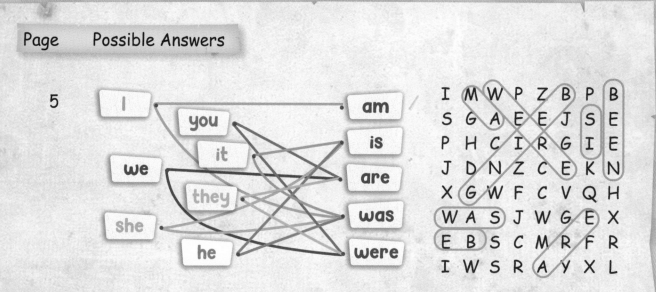

5

6-7   Bear: Can you please <u>be</u> quiet? We <u>were</u> trying to get some sleep!

Mama Bear: But now we <u>are</u> all awake!

Woodpecker: I <u>am being</u> quiet! As quiet as woodpeckers can <u>be</u>!

Baby Bear: Mr Woodpecker, I <u>am</u> very sleepy! Can you please peck on another tree?

Woman to dog: Here you <u>are</u>! I <u>was</u> looking all over for you!

Woman to dog: Where have you <u>been</u>? What <u>is</u> that all over your fur?

Woman to dog: You <u>are</u> really so naughty!

THE WONDERFUL WORLD OF WORDS

The BE Verbs

Dr Lubna Alsagoff
PhD (Stanford)

Learn English in a fun and meaningful way!

BE Family

is am be was were are being been

In this volume, children will learn about the verb "be" and its eight different forms.

Other Titles in the
Wonderful World of Words (WOW) Series